Orange Sunshine and the Psychedelic Sunrise

THE ILLUSTRATED EDITION

A Collection of Poems,
Thoughts, Reflections and Photos

Christopher Carpenter

Copyright © 2011 by Christopher Carpenter
ISBN 978-0-9887814-1-2
First Printed 2013
First Edition

www.OrangeSunshineBook.com

www.OrangeSunshineAndThePsychedelicSunrise.com

All rights reserved.
No part of this publication may be reproduced, copied, or transmitted in any form or by any means, electronic, digital or mechanical, including photography, scanning, recording, or any information storage and retrieval system, without permission in writing from Christopher Carpenter.

Printed in the United States of America
Sunshine Publishing of Clearwater

Origin of the word "Psychedelic"

"Psychedelic" derives from the Greek, meaning Soul or Mind manifesting.

In 1957, Dr. Humphrey Osmond contacted Aldous Huxley regarding a term for entheogenic experiences. In correspondence to Osmond, Huxley wrote:

"To make this mundane world sublime,
Take half a gram of phanerothyme."

Osmond responded:

"To fathom Hell or soar Angelic,
Just take a pinch of psychedelic."

Thus the term "Psychedelic" was coined.

CONTENTS

Ergo	1
Creation	2
Our Past	4
Blink of an Eye	5
For Woman with Child	6
Soul	7
The Spirit	8
Visions of Youth	9
Loneliness	10
Attraction Revealed	12
Love Search	13
The Good Way	14
DJ Messiah	16
The Christian's Dream	18
Eye of a Needle	20
The Kingdom Within	22
The Game	23
Free Will	24
Christian Rebirth	25

CONTENTS (continued)

Supreme Being	26
Freedom	27
Orange Sunshine and the Psychedelic Sunrise	28
Holy Light	30
Senses	31
Forsaken	32
Waiting	33
Bitterness	34
Regret	35
Rationalization	36
Road of Time	37
Martini Days	38
Vanity	40
Laughter	41
Slumber	42
Lucidity	43
Delirium	44
Great Ideas	45
Consciousness	46

CONTENTS (continued)

Universal Knowledge 48

Black Hole Universe 50

Intelligence 52

Arrogance 53

The City 54

Giving and Receiving 55

Kiwi Dream 56

Success and Failure 58

Life's Reason 59

Love's Desire 60

For My Love 61

Eternity Waits 62

Death 63

A Thought 64

Psychedelic Savior 65

Time's Savor 66

Perspective 67

Appendix
    Photo Locations 68

ERGO

Let us drink the fire of St. Anthony
So the Forces will battle for our Soul

Know your flesh will be eaten
Leaving your Spirit at the Core

Understand the fire of Hades
Bringing Life from death

Ancient Eleusinians
Knew the Mysteries

Celebrate
Rebirth.

CREATION

Element compressed
A star furnace
Light explodes
Darkness implodes

We are Stars
In life and death
Dust to dust
There is no rest

Eternal motion
Matter and energy
One to the other
All reality

All that was
All that is
All that will be
Star's energy

Atom Molecule Matter
Air Fire Earth Water
Heavenly mass adders

Solid Liquid Plasma Gas
Star Galaxy Universe
So vast

Time and space
Special forces and gravity
Creation's paradox
Relativity

Conscious illusion
Mind and matter
One Enlightened
Multi-verse answer

Inside outside
Within without
Orbital motion
Creation's route.

OUR PAST

Standing upright
We walk about
Not seeing our dark past

From the trees we came
With minds we sprang
To the dawn of our true Life.

BLINK OF AN EYE

Earth
Four billion years

Man
Two billion blinks

Earth sees
Fifty million generations

Man sees
The Earth blink.

FOR WOMAN WITH CHILD

The Soul holds its breath,
waiting patiently,
yearning for mortality.

Oliver Murray Carpenter and Christopher Carpenter

SOUL

The Soul is like the wind
It has no direction
If it is not moving
With the Spirit
of Emotion.

THE SPIRIT

Again, I have fallen
With the Rain
Upon the Almighty's land

Mixed with earth
A Heavenly solution
Human Soil

But the Water cleans
And the Sun shines
Again, I have risen.

VISIONS OF YOUTH

I lie here wondering in my bed
Thinking how nice it would be
If only you were here my Love
To see what I can see

With darkness all around me
The visions pass my way
Of the things that lie ahead
On that lovely day

The wind, the trees, the autumn leaves
They are all in my dreams
Where Love exists and hates extinct
In the land where no one grieves

As time passes slowly through my head
I think that I can see
Why there's only you my Love
For only We can see.

LONELINESS

Oh Love
My heart sings a song for you
May my sound have wings
To carry my melody to you

To say a word
Is to say too much
To say a thousand
Is to say less

I long for the touch of your flesh
The taste of your honey
The intoxication
Of your beauty

Ah but that which separates is only
Time and space
Let us become
One in a dream

To Live
To Love
To Be
To Become

But woe we be
If we remain separate
Alone with our words
Safe in our selves

Risking nothing
The melody not heard
My heart cries out
Knowing the cost.

ATTRACTION REVEALED

Walking on a
Wondrous day
A beauty passes
By the way

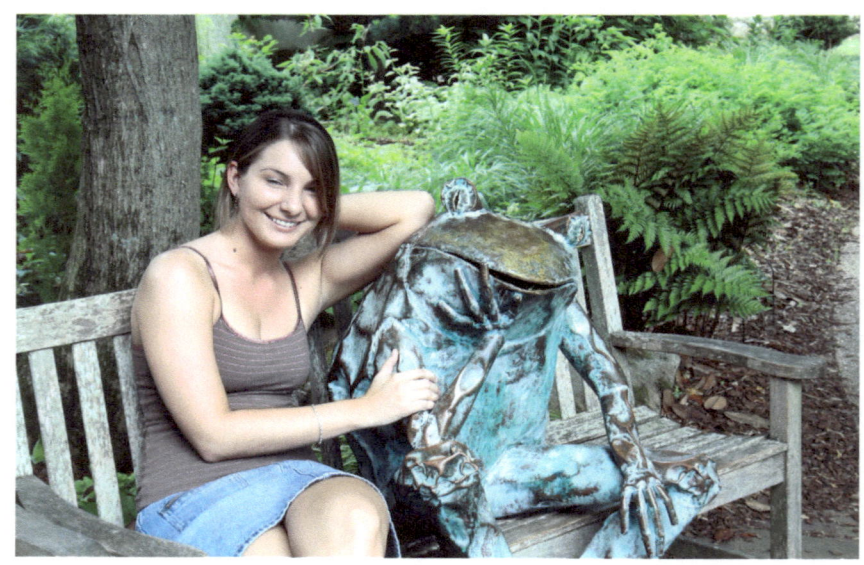

Mindful attraction
May foretell
One foot drags
Unconscious tell.

LOVE SEARCH

Divided in the now we are
Together in the past
A future hope is what we have
A Love that will forever last

The ocean's waters are like one
But rain does rise to separate
As cloud's they are free, but only to fall
As rain is our Life's fate

United as the ocean flows
To distant ports and beaches
We'll rise and fall to Love's sweet song
In search of Life's great riches

Together we shall search for Love
In a painful story
Crucified in Love's long quest
Resurrected in Love's glory.

THE GOOD WAY

Bon voyage
Molly and me
United we are
Heavenly

Food and drink
Never satisfy
Hunger for One
Will not deny

Listen closely
You will hear
Universe's heart beat
Now so near

Thousands join
March as One
Hear the same tune
Towards the Sun

Lightening bolt
Out of the blue
Divine Consciousness
Being's a rue.

DJ MESSIAH

He'll save your Soul
With rock and roll

The vinyl spins
The earth revolves
Sounds flow
Minds evolve

Timothy Leary's dead
Is the refrain
He'll take you to
The Astral Plain

Yes, go through the Door
You're close to the edge
The Mind's abyss
Relax, Flow over the ledge

Hear Heaven's beat
Across the universe
Time stands still
Angels' converse

Tomorrow never knows
Tibetan dream
Secret of Being
Listen to the Stream

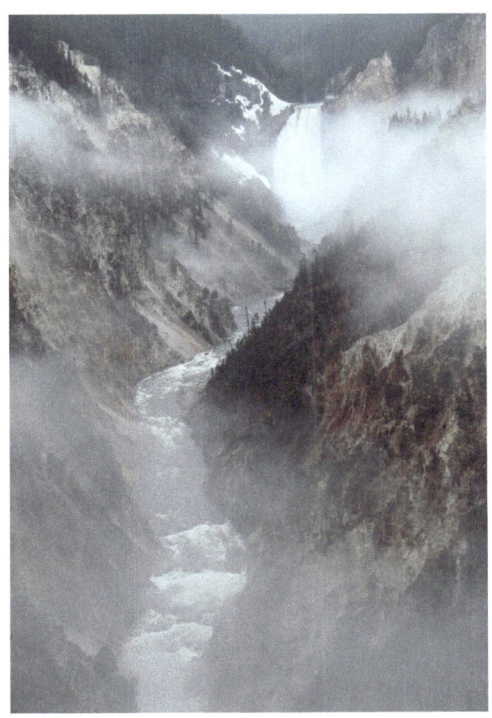

What was lost
Is Now found
The Clear Light
All around

He'll save your Soul
With rock and roll.

THE CHRISTIAN'S DREAM

The day is almost here
When they'll rise with glory
As the trumpet's play
Starring in resurrection's story

It won't be long
It won't be very long

So stay awake and watchful
and do not turn your head
Keep your eyes upon the path
and take it step by step

It won't be long
It won't be very long

Listen to those who speak
of love and harmony
Not to those of violence
Filled with acrimony

It won't be long
It won't be very long

So watch for them of power
and follow not their tricks
But watch for Him who watches
Upon the clouds so thick

It won't be long
It won't be very long.

EYE OF A NEEDLE

Hello Mr. Jones

Tree of Wealth
Fruit of Power
Corruption

Seeking Treasures
Material world
Sees evil

But not your own
For the world
Fills your eyes

You shall not find
If you know not
What to seek

You shall not receive
If you ask
For yourself alone

You shall not have the door opened
If your hands are too full
To knock

Goodbye Mr. Jones.

THE KINGDOM WITHIN

Hades road is open
Blinding misery
Kingdom's material abbey
Devoid of energy

Heaven's gate is open
For all who want to see
Mindful of the Glory
Now is time to Be.

THE GAME

Righteous is
No better man
Then the sinner is the worse

The testing game   The testing game
He played   He played
And lost   And won
        Life and Death
The other not   The other not
But if he'd played   But if he'd played
No better off   No worse off

The sinner acts
He tried the game
The righteous refrained
He never played.

FREE WILL

Mind and Body
Both are One
But who is
Slave and Master?

Pleasure's game
Body's pain
Spirit's high
Self denied.

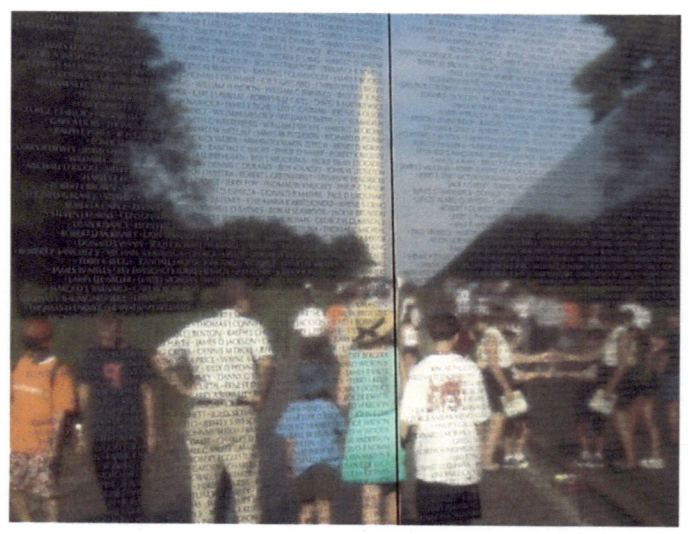

Babylon insists
People resist
Self's domain
Who will reign?

Good and Bad
Choice forbade
Choice removed
Soul disapproved.

CHRISTIAN REBIRTH

Christ submits
Masochistic pleasures

Powers crucify
Sadistic desires

Destiny embraced
The Master submits

Unknown actions
Slaves commit

Death for sin
Life for belief

Soul reborn
Eternal relief.

SUPREME BEING

So you say Freedom rings
Above the church's steeple
But who can hear for preacher's screams
Have deafened most the people

Defying Freedom's call

So you say that Heaven waits
Above the cloudy sky
But who can see for man's towers
Tears now cloud our eyes

Defying Heaven's call

Yes or no
Will we grow?

Clearing ear and eye

Yes or no
Will we know?

The Being of the Sky.

FREEDOM

A man
A mind
A thought
A word

Knowledge does come
To be

Action
Experience

Understanding brings Light
To Thee

Awareness
Heaven

The Truth
Shall set you Free.

ORANGE SUNSHINE AND THE PSYCHEDELIC SUNRISE

Knowledge burns inside
From swallowing the Sun
In anticipation
Of what is to come

The Holy One's
Gradual ascent
Clear Light
In the body's convent

Patterns imposed
Secrets disclosed

Sounds seen
Light heard

Being, seeing, believing

Time suspended
The world upended

Now is Here
Here is Now

Wall's breathe
Mysteries perceived

Unending time
Infinite space
Captured moment
Divine Grace

Reborn with caveman eyes
In Dawn's event
Consciousness revealed
Star of the Firmament

Brilliant Orange
The Mind shines
On the Psychedelic
Sunrise.

HOLY LIGHT

Gazing upon the smell of a rose
A thought grows to taste the color
The red blood of our King

Only He could understand the splendor
Living by the Light
of a rose.

SENSES

The hand writes
But cannot feel
The emotion of the heart

The eyes read
But cannot see
The knowledge of the mind

Alas, if only
Eyes could write and
Hands could see

From the outside in
Knowledge and emotion
Light and understanding.

FORSAKEN

I cry in my wisdom
and laugh in my despair
Sometimes I wonder
If I'm truly aware

For when I do ponder
I find myself lacking
In fruits of the Spirit
I'm not really bearing.

WAITING

Appointment's time is now long past
and waiting is in vain

The problem's known
But not the cure
and so there is the pain.

BITTERNESS

Crucified on a cross of time,
by memories that are not mine.

Forgive?
Forget?
I ask why?

I know!
I will!
When I die!

REGRET

Stabbed in the heart
With an ice pick of thought

Emotion's heat melts away
Memories of pain

Reason feels
Time heals.

RATIONALIZATION

So they say Reason is welcome,
but who do they fool?

For they are strangers
and rationalization is the tool.

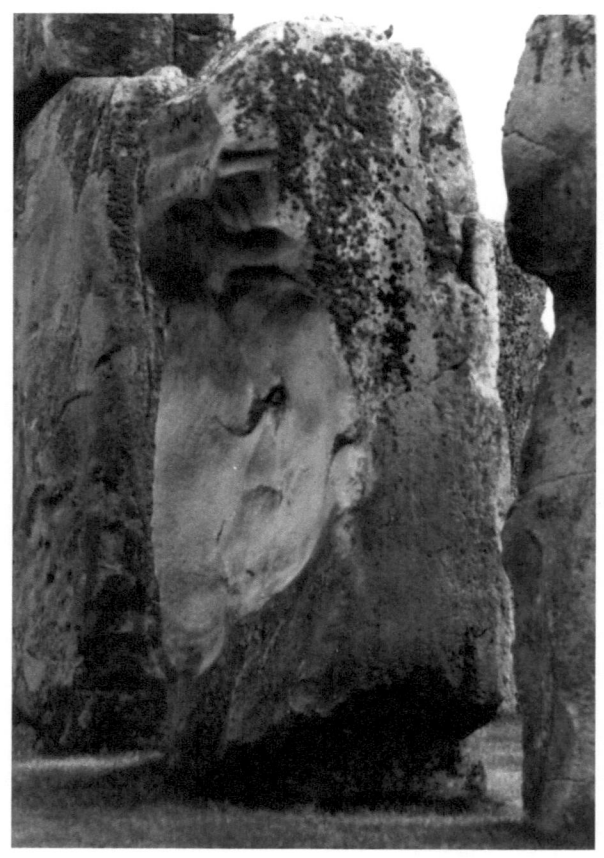

To save our dear House
we must open the Blinds.

Look upon the face of Truth,
The Good Samaritan in Time!

ROAD OF TIME

Traveling down the road of Time
Knowing not the goal
Wondering if I missed a sign
On this road of mine

Looking back upon the past
Seeing where I've been
Wondering how it went so fast
On this road of mine

Standing in the present now
With so many paths to follow
Wondering if I'll reach the Land
On this road of mine

Seeing not what future be
For it is all too dark
Wondering what will become of me
On this road of mine

So I'll keep rounding every bend
With Faith my silent keeper
Knowing that there will be no end
On this road of mine.

MARTINI DAYS

Have another drink
My friend
We all die of something
In the end

Eyes see
The sunset of life

Resisting the day
Holding on to the past
Nothing lasts

Eternal
Lights dance on the sea
Shimmering to be free

Life's
Sunset approaches
Human reproaches

Age advances
Foregone chances
Tears fall
Like the rain

If only I could
Turn back time
Rewrite the past
Make it mine

Martini daze
Numbs the pain.

VANITY

You see what you want to see
Self fulfilling prophesy.

LAUGHTER

A little laughter
Every day
Will resist
Insanity

And if it doesn't
What the hey
We had some fun
Along the way.

SLUMBER

Sandman's pallet
Paints the world
Mind's surprise
Will unfurl

Renaissance colors
Light the Sky
Soft, pink pillows
Fill thine eyes

Marble halls
Hold Heaven's gate
World of dreams
Marvels await.

LUCIDITY

Angels and Demons
Fairies too
Messengers in Heaven
From me to you.

Are you there?
Do you feel the same?
Here my Love
There is no shame.

Dream's warmth
Feels so good
When shared with you
They are understood.

Awake in sleep
Orchestrated fantasy
Minds to reap
Boundless reality.

DELIRIUM

Knocking Knocking
At Heaven's gate
Memories fade
From Life's parade

Mind fails
In the body's jail
Ravages of time
Not benign

Life forgotten
Dreams begotten

Real or imagined
Mind separates
Dreams escape
Reality's gate

Walls come down
Confusion abounds
Dreams remembered
Reality dismembered.

GREAT IDEAS

Sand castles
Mindful shores
Washed away
Time ignores

Launched ships
Serendipity's time
Safe from tides
Idea sublime.

CONSCIOUSNESS

A beautiful Melody never Heard
Remains so
If not discovered

All things
Exist
In Space and Time

Known and Unknown
Discovered and Undiscovered
Learned and Created

The Mind seeks and finds
Leaping from the Known
to the Unknown

Learning
The Mind Discovers
The Known

Creating
The Mind Discovers
The Unknown

Consciousness Aware
In Space and Time
The Unknown to Known

A beautiful Melody
Exists to Be
Heard.

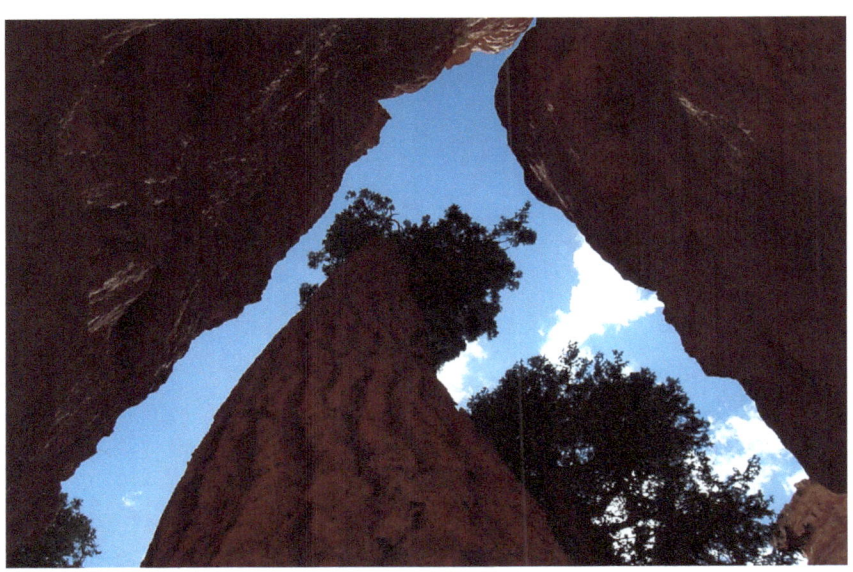

UNIVERSAL KNOWLEDGE

Building
Mind by mind
Accumulating
Over all time

Geocentric
Philosophy
Earth center
Natural folly

Ancient's pretender
Math contorted
Perverted defender
Religion supported

Sun centers
Celestial spheres
In revolution
No one hears

Orbits observed
Heresy deserved
House arrest
Truth's oppressed

Dialogue solution
Scientific revolution
Universal controversy
Religious impossibility

Natural laws
Math philosophy
Motion and gravity
Principled certainty

Mass and light
Energy
Time and space
Relativity

Strong and weak
Ideas compete
Expanding knowledge
Mankind's homage.

BLACK HOLE UNIVERSE

Alpha Void

Singularity's abode
Darkness explodes
Light exposed

Zero and one
Yes and No
Light and dark
That's all we know

Bigger and bigger
Larger and larger
So it grows
To its ultimate repose

Universe consumed
Black appetite
No more light

Inside out
New universe
In reverse

Light implodes
Darkness imposed
Singularity's abode

Omega Void.

INTELLIGENCE

Intelligence in
Jeopardy
Same as you, same as me
Artificial similarity.

Consciousness, Thought
Being's aware
Beauty, Humor
Originality's fare.

Create or simulate
Given a test
Independence
Will attest.

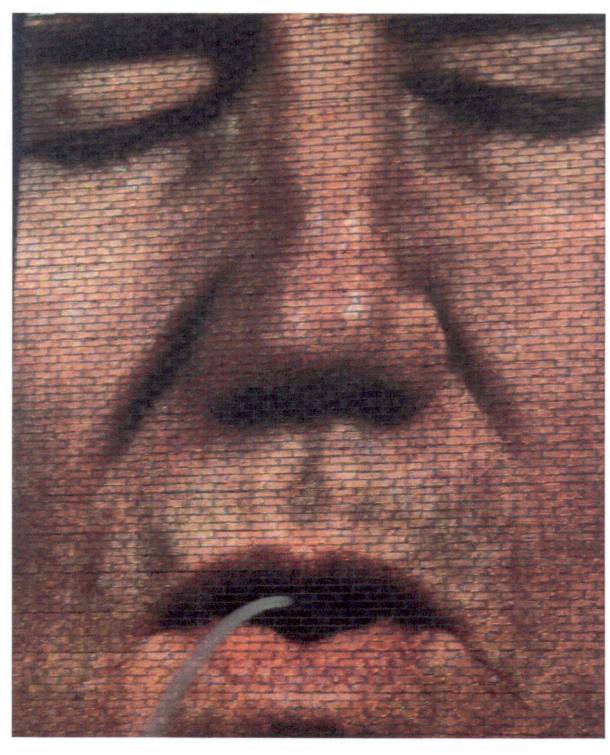

ARROGANCE

Tick tock
Man made clocks

Four billion years
Twenty four nadirs

Garden of Eden
Apple Eaten

Man is God - God is Man

Omnipotent Power
The world deflowered

Four seconds
Man's descendants

Climate changed
Man deranged.

THE CITY

Sprawling metro
Population soars
Green is gone
Concrete galore

Nature glows
Life's energy
City dwellers
Can not see

City living misses
Night sky's beauty
Losing touch
With nature's glory.

GIVING AND RECEIVING

The sun shines
The wind blows
The rain falls
The earth glows.

KIWI DREAM

Sky's sword
Earth's reward
In the Land of Rainbows

Land shakes
Humans awake
In the Land of Rainbows

Barefoot days
Heavens ablaze
In the Land of Rainbows

Native tears
Frozen glaciers
In the Land of Rainbows

Ice age retreat
Fjords greet
In the Land of Rainbows

Hunters' instinct
Prey extinct
In the Land of Rainbows

Flightless bird
Life preserved
In the Land of Rainbows

Golden fruit
Taste suits
In the Land of Rainbows

Bungee jumps
Hearts' thump
In the Land of Rainbows

Enchanting hills
Orb thrills
In the Land of Rainbows

Green stone
Spirit's own
In the Land of Rainbows

Water impacts
Light refracts
In the Land of Rainbows

Beautiful sounds
Treasures abound
In the Land of Rainbows.

SUCCESS AND FAILURE

Nothing silences the critics
Better than success

Failure opens their mouths
With an even greater chorus.

LIFE'S REASON

Love's seed did grow between us
In fertile soil it laid
Watered when our tears did fall
Warmed in Love's embrace

It grew so slow around us
Like the clock's long march through time
Blossomed in the darkest night
And the sunrise in our morn

It stood the weather, good and bad
In storms it held like rock
And in the warm and sunny days
Our plant became a lock

To hold us till the end of Time
In our Lover's prison
Till God relieves us of our Lives
From Life's best reason.

LOVE'S DESIRE

Caged heart
Bleeds profusely

Tears burn
Open Wounds

The flesh is
Divine
Intoxication.

FOR MY LOVE

Does the waning moon,
Know that Life with Love,
Flows and ebbs, too fast, too soon?

Oliver Murray Carpenter and Christopher Carpenter

ETERNITY WAITS

The tide of Time
Ebbs and flows
The dry Land
Yearns for Water

My Soul
Drifts with longing
Stagnant
It gathers dead thoughts

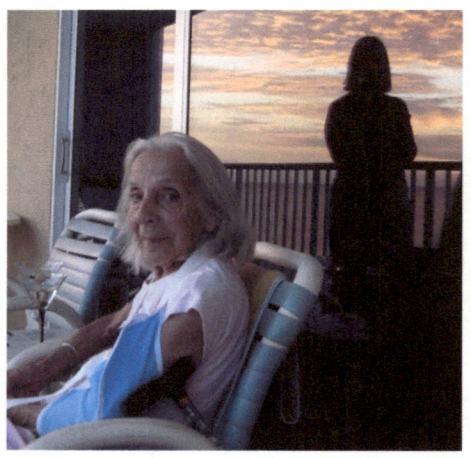

The erosion
of mind
Takes place over time
Infinity is patient

Laughing we see
Futility
of finite self

Crying we see
Joy
of Eternity.

DEATH

Death is Life unmasked
Don't behold His Face aghast
Soul will ever last.

A THOUGHT

A hint
The birds awake
A gentle song
Silence abates

Anticipation
A hue of pink
A thought awakes

Rising slow
With so much grace
Glowing high
It takes its place.

PSYCHEDELIC SAVIOR

The colors swirled
Into the psychedelic vortex
From which they sprang

Leaving One
Crystallized Thought
Life

So it must Be

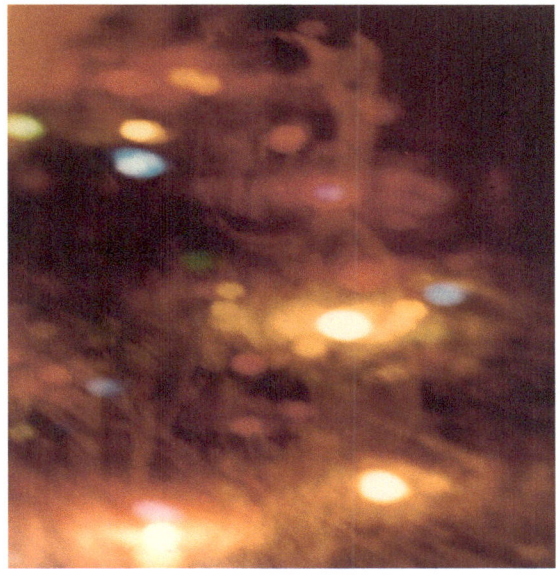

One Thought
One Creation
One Essence

Revelation of Self
The Savior rises
With Knowledge

Being.

TIME'S SAVOR

Time is fleeting
So they say
So do not waste
A single day

Seize the moment
Squeeze it tight
Savor every drop
Experience its delight.

PERSPECTIVE

I would like to Be

A blade of grass
On a hill
With a mountain
Rising high
On the horizon
Below the sun
That is setting
On the day
That I die

I would like to Be.

APPENDIX
Photo Locations

Arrogance: Yellowstone National Park, Wyoming
A Thought: Satellite Beach, Florida
Attraction Revealed: Botanical Garden, Atlanta, Georgia
Bitterness: Yellowstone National Park, Wyoming
Black Hole Universe: Yellowstone National Park, Wyoming
Blink of an Eye: Mesa Verde National Park, Colorado
Christian Rebirth: Mosaic, Venice, Italy
Consciousness: Bryce Canyon National Park, Utah
Creation: Yellowstone National Park, Wyoming
Death: Arlington National Cemetery, Arlington, Virginia
Delirium: Yellowstone National Park, Wyoming
DJ Messiah: Yellowstone National Park, Wyoming
Ergo: Indian Shores, Florida
Eternity Waits: Indian Shores, Florida
Eye of a Needle: New York, New York and Las Vegas, Nevada
For My Love: Indian Shores, Florida
Forsaken: Great Sand Dunes National Park, Colorado
For Woman with Child: Shedd Aquarium, Chicago, Illinois
Freedom: Baird Glacier, Alaska
Free Will: Vietnam Veterans Memorial, Washington, D.C.
Giving and Receiving: Mt. Le Conte, Tennessee
Great Ideas: Indian Shores, Florida and New York, New York
Holy Light: Water Color Painting by Christopher Carpenter
Intelligence: Crown Fountain, Chicago, Illinois
Kiwi Dream: Napier, New Zealand
Laughter: Great Smoky Mountains National Park, Tennessee
Life's Reason: Kyoto, Japan
Loneliness: Milford Sound, New Zealand and
    Greymouth, New Zealand
Love's Desire: Venice, Italy
Love Search: Botanical Gardens, Nevis, Lesser Antilles
Lucidity: Baird Glacier, Alaska
Martini Days: Indian Shores, Florida

APPENDIX
Photo Locations (continued)

Orange Sunshine and the Psychedelic Sunrise:
    Satellite Beach, Florida
Our Past: Monolith from 2001: A Space Odyssey,
    Stanley Kubrick Exhibition,
    Los Angeles County Museum of Art
Perspective: Kaikoura, New Zealand
Psychedelic Savior: Christmas Tree, Royal Palm Beach, Florida
Rationalization: Stonehenge, England
Regret: Mendenhall Glacier, Alaska
Road of Time: Monument Valley, Utah
Senses: Cloud Gate, Millennium Park, Chicago, Illinois
Slumber: Grand Canyon National Park, Arizona
Soul: Yellowstone National Park, Wyoming
Success and Failure: Wiesbaden, Germany and Kyoto, Japan
Supreme Being: Nevis, Lesser Antilles
The Christian's Dream: Greymouth, New Zealand and
    Oliver Cromwell, House of Commons, London, England
The City: Chicago, Illinois
The Game: Las Vegas, Nevada
The Good Way: Venice, Italy
The Kingdom Within: Tintern Abbey, Wales
The Spirit: Grand Canyon National Park, Arizona
Time's Savor: Santa Fe, New Mexico
Universal Knowledge: Valley of the Kings and Giza, Egypt
Vanity: Chicago, Illinois
Visions of Youth: Mt. Dewey, Wrangell, Alaska
Waiting: Grand Canyon National Park, Arizona

All photos Copyright © by Christopher Carpenter